# [Imprint]
MAKE YOUR MARK

A part of Macmillan Publishing Group, LLC
175 Fifth Avenue, New York, NY 10010

Library of Congress Cataloging-in-Publication Data is available.

ISBN 978-1-250-22093-6 (hardcover) / ISBN 978-1-250-22094-3 (ebook)

Our books may be purchased in bulk for promotional, educational, or business use. Please contact your
local bookseller or the Macmillan Corporate and Premium Sales Department at (800) 221-7945
ext. 5442 or by email at MacmillanSpecialMarkets@macmillan.com.

Book design by Natalie C. Sousa

Imprint logo designed by Amanda Spielman

First edition, 2018

1 3 5 7 9 10 8 6 4 2

If you steal this book,
you will suffer both barks and bites . . .
especially early in the mornings.

# FIRE
## AND
# FURRY

## PETS GET POLITICAL

EDITED BY

# MICHAEL WOOF

**{Imprint}**
MAKE YOUR MARK

NEW YORK

# HE MIGHT PEE ON YOU.

# KITTENS SCRATCH BACK.

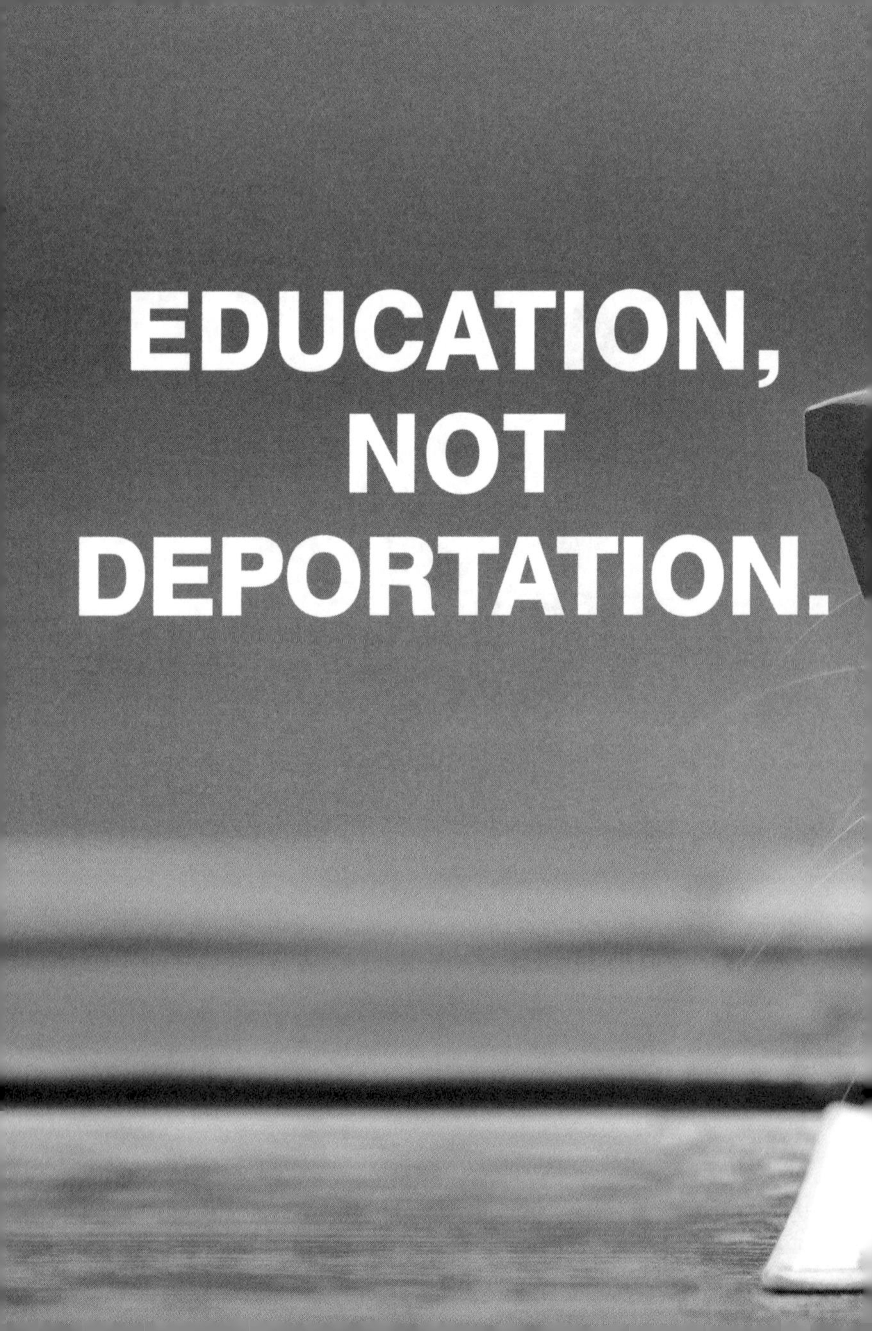
EDUCATION,
NOT
DEPORTATION.

# FAKE MEWS!

# JOIN THE RE-*HISS*-TANCE!

PETIZENS UNITE!

# TWITTER IS NOT POLICY.

# WATCHING THE NEWS FEELS LIKE...

# RECLAIMING MY TIME.

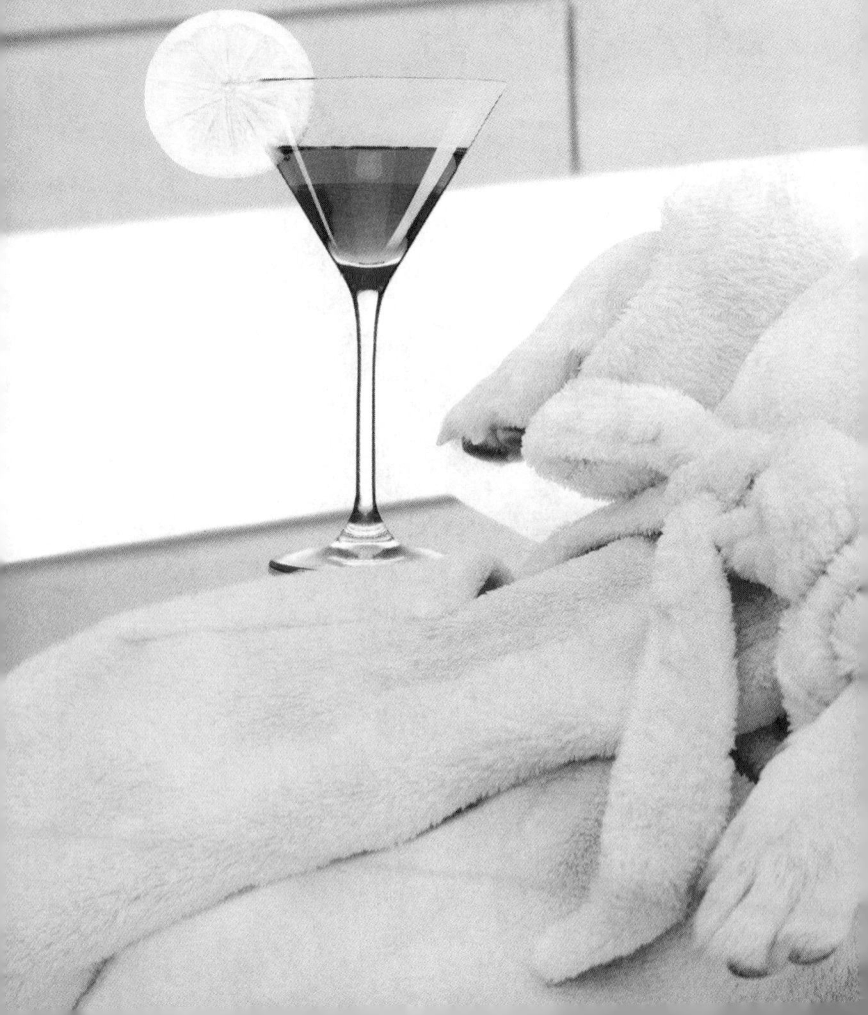

# SO MUCH COLLUSION.

# THERE IS NO PEE TAPE.

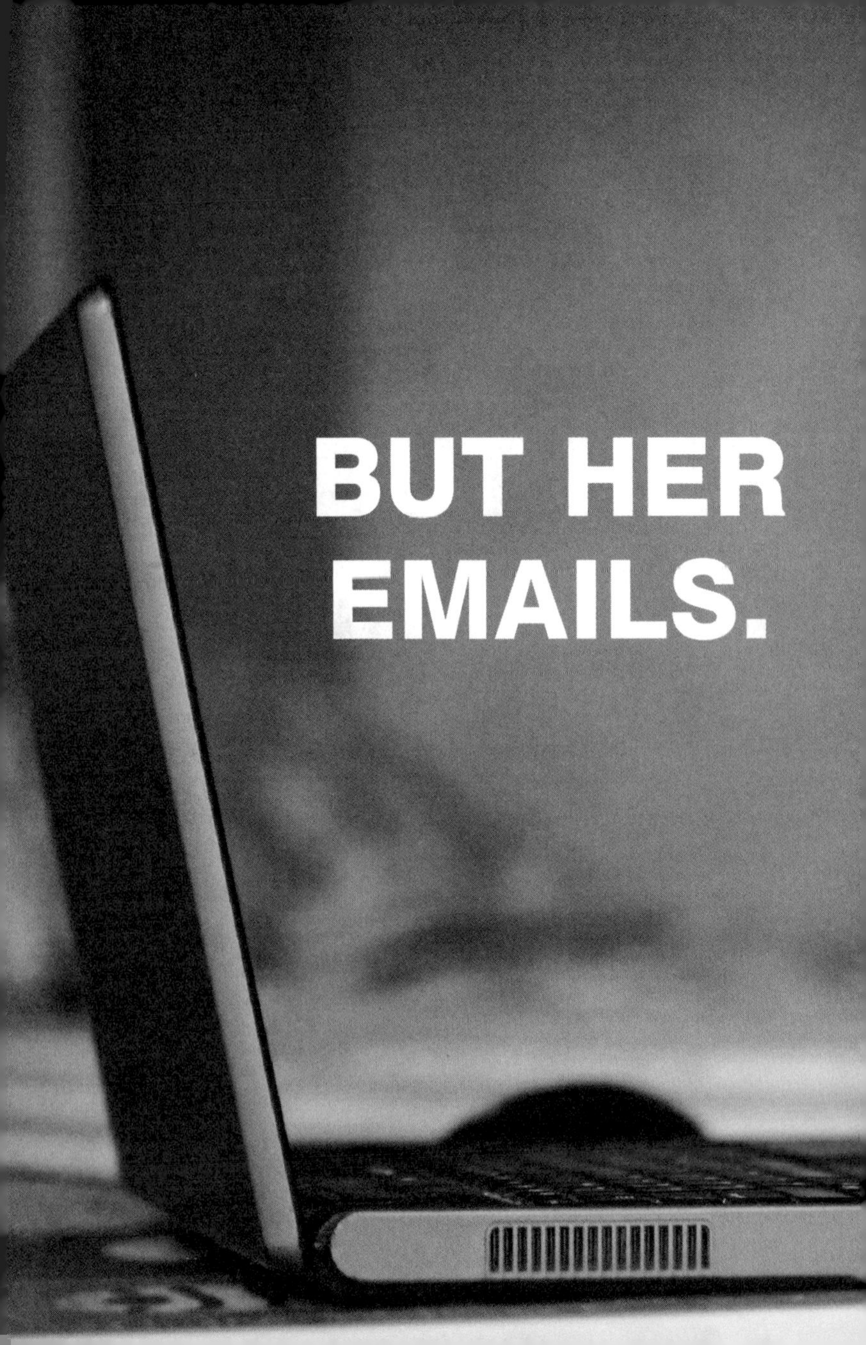
BUT HER
EMAILS.

I THOUGHT IT WOULD BE EASIER.

RISE UP

AND RESIST.

HE'S BEEN A VERY BAD DOG, A VERY UNFAIR DOG.

HE'S REALLY A VERY BAD DOG.

CONFIDENTIAL

HE KNOWS
HE'S A
BAD DOG.

THIS IS MY
REAL HAIR.

FOX . . .

# I DON'T READ FAKE NEWS.

lrstyles
lair?
UL STYLISTS

ts

or

# IT TAKES ALL KINDS.

**PUSSY PARTY.**

# NOT MY PRESIDENT.

YOU'RE
FIRED!

# CAN'T BUILD A WALL.

# HANDS TOO SMALL.

# WAKE ME WHEN IT'S OVER.

**MAKE LOVE, NOT WAR.**

# USE YOUR BARK!

# RESIST.

# POWER
# TO THE
# PUPPIES.

AT DAWN,
WE RISE.

# DRAIN THE SWAMP.

**MODEL DIPLOMACY.**

# BIGGEST CROWD EVER.

# THIS IS WHAT DEMOCRACY LOOKS LIKE.

# SWING VOTE.

# ALTERNATIVE FACTS.

# THE ONLY FOX WORTH WATCHING.

# SHE'S A POLICY HAWK.

# GET OUT THE VOTE.

# EQUAL BITES FOR ALL.

# MAKE ANIMALS *GRRR*-EAT AGAIN.

# YUGE.

# DON'T TWEET.
# VOTE.

# I'M
# WITH
# HER.

# GET
# ORGANIZED.

# I REALLY DO CARE.

# DO YOU?

MY BODY.
MY CHOICE.

# CAT-IVIST.

# HEAR US ROAR!

# I HAVE MANY KITTENS.

# SO MANY KITTENS.

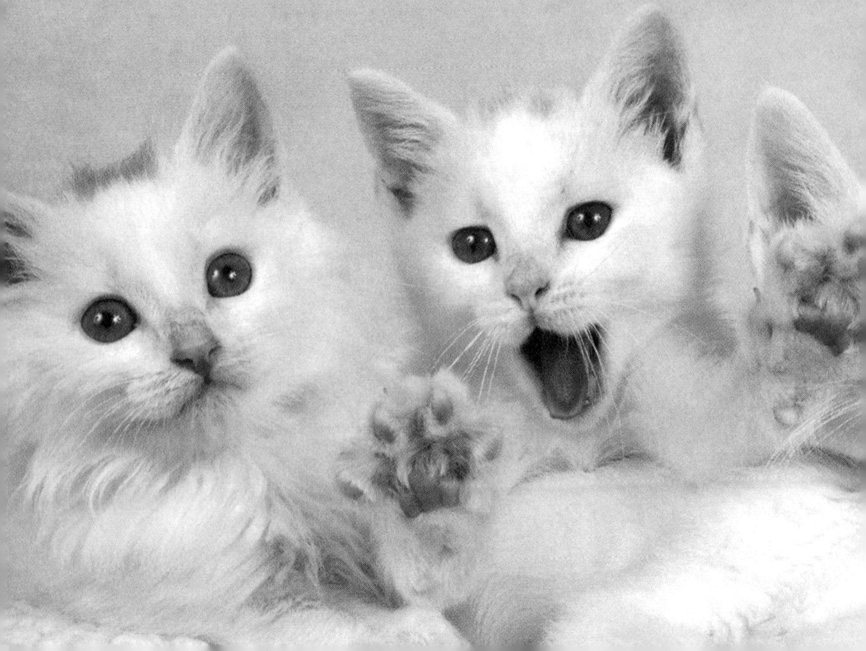

# I HAVE
# SO MANY
# KITTENS.

# THE FUTURE
# IS FELINE.

# SPACE
# FORCE.

# I CAN PARDON MYSELF.

**SAD!**

# ALL BARK
# AND
# NO BITE.

# TINY HANDS.

BUILD A BRIDGE, NOT A WALL.

# ALL ARE WELCOME.

# BORDER COLLIES, NOT BORDERS.

FAMILIES
BELONG
TOGETHER.

# LOVE IS LOVE!

# PUPPY
# PRIDE.

# GLOBAL WARMING IS REAL.

# SAVE THE PLANET!

# HEALTH
# CARE
# FOR ALL!

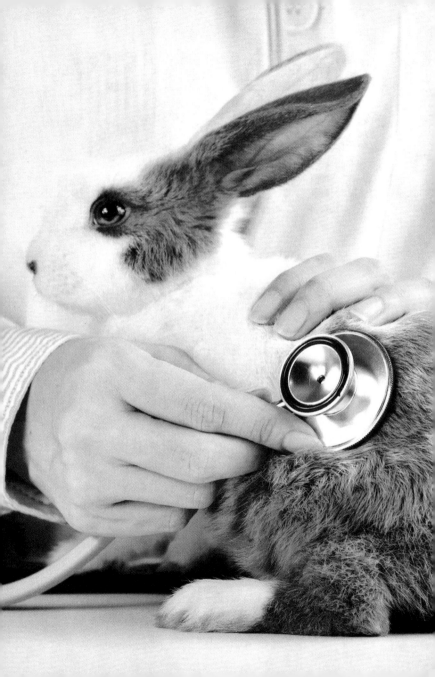

# WHEN THEY GO LOW, WE GO HIGH.

# I VOTED!

# KEEP HOPE ALIVE.

# TAKING A TWITTER BREAK.

NEVERTHELESS,

# SHE PERSISTED.

# STRONGER
# TOGETHER.

# STAY WOKE.